The Daily Haiku Writer

The Daily Haiku Writer

A Mindfulness Poetry Journal

The PLAYHARD Press

Asheville Bellingham Ithaca

Foreword

There are moments in your life that stay with you ever after. The way a leaf in autumn lingers, slowly slipping to the ground, or how the full-moon reflects off the water on a still summer night—these intimate moments of connection bring you closer to knowing yourself and the world around you. They make you mindful of the present moment and bring awareness to your life. Sharing your unique experience is the very heart of haiku. This workbook companion to the bestselling book *The Daily Haiku Reader* is your journal for poetic expression.

There is no wrong way to write haiku. Many people might identify haiku as a seventeen-syllable poem with lines of five, seven, and five syllables. Although commonly taught and widely accepted, this simple definition omits the nuance and subtlety for which the haiku writing tradition is revered. Capturing the essence of a single moment that touches your heart is the true spirit of haiku. Conveying those feelings to your reader is the challenge of crafting haiku. When you finally strike on the perfect diction, cadence, and mood, the rewards are infinite.

The way one crafts haiku is as unique as the individual who writes them. Whether one decides to use the challenge of counting syllables of five, seven, and five is entirely personal. Structuring poems around syllables is by no means necessary to compose outstanding haiku. Many find this form to have a balance and grace suitable to the rhythm of English, while also providing a challenge when attempting to distill the essence of a moment into haiku. Others prefer not to be burdened by the rules of meter and instead focus on simply conveying the majesty of experience.

Nature is traditionally a central feature of haiku. They often focus on the environment and follow the season cycle, as is observed by the layout of both this journal and of the *Reader*. The connection that human beings have to the natural world is a universal phenomenon, bridging generations, cultures, and gaps in centuries of time alike. The power of this connection is vast, but modern haiku often transcends this unifying element and conveys a meaning that is more closely aligned with our high-speed, modern lives. Again, the beauty and magic of haiku comes from the essence of the moment, whatever that moment may be—not necessarily the content that created it. While nature is boundless with grist for the mill, so, too, is modern life. Where you derive inspiration to conjure your lines is entirely up to you.

No matter the impetus for your writing, a few certain things are helpful to keep in the back of your mind. First, people experience the world through their five senses. These sensations rush to our brains and help us interpret our world. What starts as a sensation impulse is quickly translated into the things we feel, our mental images, and finally the words we use. When writers use language that draws directly from our senses, they forge a connection that awakens our own deep-rooted experiences. This helps us identify with the writing and makes it feel especially personal. Next, things often happen outside of ourselves and we are the ones privy to observing them. Omitting the use of personal pronouns can elevate the focus of the writing and aid in the economy of words. This can sharpen a poem's point and keep an idea on target. Last, the art of mindfulness is all about being in the here and now—not being lost in the past or projecting into the endless future. Therefore, writing haiku in the present tense helps to keep the reader in the present moment and, in turn, keeps your moment present, eternally.

The Daily Haiku Writer leads you down a path of your own awareness through the changing seasons of the year. For each day, compose a new haiku as only you can evoke it. Creating these brief, poetic reflections will serve to nourish you, enhance your mindfulness practice, and refresh your inner wellspring. The central act of haiku is capturing the essence of a sensation or event that touches you. The completion of haiku takes place in your reader's mind, where it echoes and awakens, tapping their unique memories and experiences, bridging you to your fellow human beings, and kindling your ancestral connection to the natural world. May your poetic imagination resonate with all who are invited to read your haiku.

Matthew Barrington
Winter 2023
Ithaca

The Daily Haiku Writer

January 1st

_____

_____

_____

New Year's Day

January 2nd

_____

_____

_____

_____

_____

_____

January 4th

_____

_____

_____

_____

_____

_____

January 6th

_____

_____

_____

_____

_____

_____

January 8th

_____

_____

_____

_____

_____

_____

January 10th

_____

_____

_____

January 12th

_____

_____

_____

January 14th

_____

_____

_____

January 16th

_____

_____

_____

_____

_____

_____

January 18th

_____

_____

_____

_____

_____

_____

January 20th

_____

_____

_____

Martin Luther King Jr. Day

_____

_____

_____

January 22nd

_____

_____

_____

January 23rd

_____

_____

_____

January 24th

_____

_____

_____

_____

_____

_____

January 26th

_____

_____

_____

_____

_____

_____

January 28th

_____

_____

_____

_____

_____

_____

January 30th

_____

_____

_____

_____

_____

_____

February 1st

_____

_____

_____

February 2nd

_____

_____

_____

Groundhog Day

February 3rd

_____

_____

_____

_____

_____

_____

February 5th

_____

_____

_____

February 7th

_____

_____

_____

_____

_____

_____

February 9th

_____

_____

_____

_____

_____

_____

February 11th

_____

_____

_____

_____

_____

_____

February 13th

_____

_____

_____

_____

_____

_____

St. Valentine's Day

February 15th

_____

_____

_____

_____

_____

_____

February 17th

_____

_____

_____

President's Day

_____

_____

_____

February 19th

_____

_____

_____

_____

_____

_____

February 21st

_____

_____

_____

February 23rd

_____

_____

_____

_____

_____

_____

February 25th

_____

_____

_____

February 27th

_____

_____

_____

_____

_____

_____

March 1st

_____

_____

_____

March 3rd

_____

_____

_____

_____

_____

_____

March 5th

_____

_____

_____

_____

_____

_____

March 7th

_____

_____

_____

March 9th

_____

_____

_____

March 11th

_____

_____

_____

March 13th

_____

_____

_____

March 15th

_____

_____

_____

March 17th

_____

_____

_____

St. Patrick's Day

_____

_____

_____

March 19th

_____

_____

_____

_____

_____

_____

March 21st

_____

_____

_____

March 23rd

_____

_____

_____

_____

_____

_____

March 25th

_____

_____

_____

_____

_____

_____

March 27th

_____

_____

_____

March 29th

_____

_____

_____

_____

_____

_____

March 31st

_____

_____

_____

_____

_____

_____

April Fool's Day

April 2nd

_____

_____

_____

_____

_____

_____

April 4th

_____

_____

_____

_____

_____

_____

April 6th

_____

_____

_____

April 8th

_____

_____

_____

_____

_____

_____

April 10th

_____

_____

_____

_____

_____

_____

April 12th

_____

_____

_____

April 14th

_____

_____

_____

_____

_____

_____

April 16th

_____

_____

_____

April 18th

_____

_____

_____

April 20th

April 22nd

_____

_____

_____

Earth Day

_____

_____

_____

April 24th

_____

_____

_____

April 26th

_____

_____

_____

_____

_____

_____

April 28th

_____

_____

_____

April 30th

_____

_____

_____

_____

_____

_____

May 2nd

_____

_____

_____

May 4th

_____

_____

_____

_____

_____

_____

Cinco de Mayo

May 6th

_____

_____

_____

_____

_____

_____

May 8th

_____

_____

_____

_____

_____

_____

May 10th

_____

_____

_____

_____

_____

_____

May 12th

_____

_____

_____

_____

_____

_____

May 14th

_____

_____

_____

_____

_____

_____

May 16th

_____

_____

_____

_____

_____

_____

May 18th

_____

_____

_____

_____

_____

_____

May 20th

_____

_____

_____

May 22nd

_____

_____

_____

_____

_____

_____

May 24th

_____

_____

_____

_____

_____

_____

May 26th

_____

_____

_____

May 28th

_____

_____

_____

May 30th

_____

_____

_____

_____

_____

_____

June 1st

_____

_____

_____

_____

_____

_____

June 3rd

_____

_____

_____

_____

_____

_____

June 5th

_____

_____

_____

_____

_____

_____

June 7th

_____

_____

_____

_____

_____

_____

June 9th

_____

_____

_____

June 10th

_____

_____

_____

June 11th

_____

_____

_____

_____

_____

_____

June 13th

June 15th

_____

_____

_____

_____

_____

_____

June 17th

_____

_____

_____

_____

_____

_____

June 19th

_____

_____

_____

_____

_____

_____

June 21st

_____

_____

_____

June 23rd

_____

_____

_____

_____

_____

_____

June 25th

_____

_____

_____

_____

_____

_____

June 27th

_____

_____

_____

June 29th

_____

_____

_____

_____

_____

_____

July 1st

_____

_____

_____

_____

_____

_____

July 3rd

_____

_____

_____

_____

_____

_____

Independence Day

July 5th

_____

_____

_____

_____

_____

_____

July 7th

_____

_____

_____

July 8th

_____

_____

_____

July 9th

_____

_____

_____

_____

_____

_____

July 11th

_____

_____

_____

_____

_____

_____

July 13th

_____

_____

_____

July 15th

_____

_____

_____

_____

_____

_____

July 17th

_____

_____

_____

July 19th

_____

_____

_____

_____

_____

_____

July 21st

_____

_____

_____

_____

_____

_____

July 23rd

_____

_____

_____

_____

_____

_____

July 25th

_____

_____

_____

_____

_____

_____

July 27th

_____

_____

_____

_____

_____

_____

July 29th

_____

_____

_____

July 31st

_____

_____

_____

_____

_____

_____

August 2nd

_____

_____

_____

_____

_____

_____

August 4th

_____

_____

_____

_____

_____

_____

August 6th

_____

_____

_____

_____

_____

_____

August 8th

_____

_____

_____

_____

_____

_____

August 10th

_____

_____

_____

August 12th

_____

_____

_____

_____

_____

_____

August 14th

_____

_____

_____

_____

_____

_____

August 16th

_____

_____

_____

_____

_____

_____

August 18th

_____

_____

_____

_____

_____

_____

August 20th

_____

_____

_____

_____

_____

_____

August 22nd

_____

_____

_____

_____

_____

_____

August 24th

_____

_____

_____

_____

_____

_____

August 26th

_____

_____

_____

August 28th

_____

_____

_____

August 30th

_____

_____

_____

_____

_____

_____

September 1st

_____

_____

_____

_____

_____

_____

September 3rd

_____

_____

_____

_____

_____

_____

September 5th

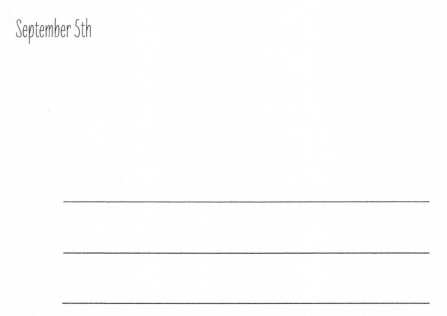

_____

_____

_____

September 7th

_____

_____

_____

_____

_____

_____

September 9th

September 11th

_____

_____

_____

9/11 Remembrance Day

September 13th

_____

_____

_____

_____

_____

_____

September 15th

_____

_____

_____

_____

_____

_____

September 17th

_____

_____

_____

September 19th

_____

_____

_____

_____

_____

_____

September 21st

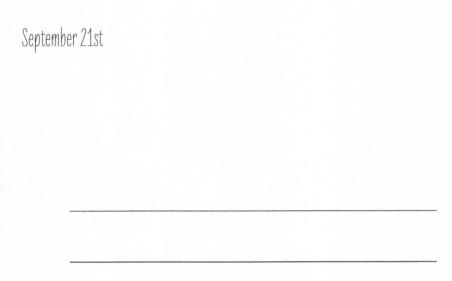

_____

_____

_____

September 23rd

_____

_____

_____

_____

_____

_____

September 25th

_____

_____

_____

September 27th

_____

_____

_____

September 29th

_____

_____

_____

_____

_____

_____

October 1st

_____

_____

_____

October 3rd

_____

_____

_____

October 5th

_____

_____

_____

October 7th

_____

_____

_____

_____

_____

_____

October 9th

_____

_____

_____

October 11th

_____

_____

_____

_____

_____

_____

October 13th

_____

_____

_____

October 15th

_____

_____

_____

October 17th

_____

_____

_____

October 19th

_____

_____

_____

_____

_____

_____

October 21st

_____

_____

_____

_____

_____

_____

October 23rd

_____

_____

_____

October 25th

_____

_____

_____

October 27th

_____

_____

_____

October 29th

_____

_____

_____

_____

_____

_____

October 31st

_____

_____

_____

Halloween

November 2nd

_____

_____

_____

_____

_____

_____

November 4th

_____

_____

_____

_____

_____

_____

November 6th

_____

_____

_____

November 8th

_____

_____

_____

_____

_____

_____

November 10th

_____

_____

_____

_____

_____

_____

Veteran's Day

November 12th

_____

_____

_____

November 14th

November 16th

_____

_____

_____

_____

_____

_____

November 18th

_____

_____

_____

November 20th

November 22nd

_____

_____

_____

November 24th

November 26th

_____

_____

_____

_____

_____

_____

November 28th

_____

_____

_____

November 30th

_____

_____

_____

_____

_____

_____

December 2nd

_____

_____

_____

_____

_____

_____

December 4th

_____

_____

_____

_____

_____

_____

December 6th

_____

_____

_____

_____

_____

_____

Pearl Harbor Day

December 8th

_____

_____

_____

_____

_____

_____

December 10th

_____

_____

_____

December 12th

_____

_____

_____

December 13th

_____

_____

_____

December 14th

_____

_____

_____

_____

_____

_____

December 16th

_____

_____

_____

December 18th

_____

_____

_____

_____

_____

_____

December 20th

_____

_____

_____

December 22nd

_____

_____

_____

_____

_____

_____

December 24th

_____

_____

_____

_____

_____

_____

Christmas Day

December 26th

_____

_____

_____

December 28th

_____

_____

_____

December 30th

_____

_____

_____

December 31st

_____

_____

_____

New Year's Eve

Made in the USA
Las Vegas, NV
02 October 2024

96115398R00218